LONDON'S WATERWAYS

Exploring the capital's rivers and canals

LONDON'S WATERWAYS

Exploring the capital's rivers and canals

DEREK PRATT

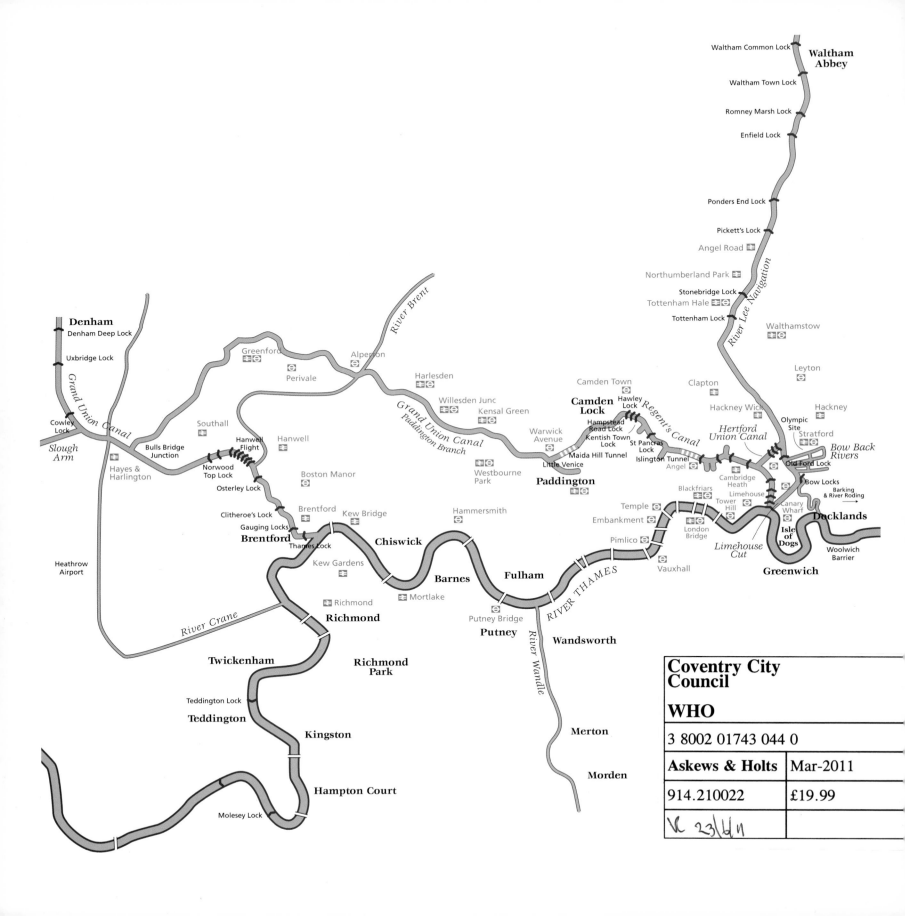

Waltham Common Lock
Waltham Abbey
Waltham Town Lock
Romney Marsh Lock
Enfield Lock
Ponders End Lock
Pickett's Lock
Angel Road
Northumberland Park
Stonebridge Lock
Tottenham Hale
Tottenham Lock
River Lee Navigation
Walthamstow
Leyton
Clapton
Hackney Wick
Hackney
Hertford Union Canal
Olympic Site
Stratford
Bow Back Rivers
Old Ford Lock
Bow Locks
Barking & River Roding
Cambridge Heath
Docklands
Canary Wharf
Isle of Dogs
Woolwich Barrier
Greenwich
Limehouse Cut
Limehouse
Tower Hill
London Bridge
Blackfriars
Temple
Embankment
Pimlico
Vauxhall

River Brent
Denham
Denham Deep Lock
Uxbridge Lock
Greenford
Perivale
Alperton
Harlesden
Camden Town
Camden Lock
Hawley Lock
Regent's Canal
Willesden Junc
Kensal Green
Hampstead Road Lock
Kentish Town Lock
St Pancras Lock
Warwick Avenue
Maida Hill Tunnel
Little Venice
Islington Tunnel
Angel
Grand Union Canal
Cowley Lock
Grand Union Canal
Southall
Hanwell
Hanwell Flight
Norwood Top Lock
Osterley Lock
Clitheroe's Lock
Gauging Locks
Brentford
Thames Lock
Slough Arm
Bulls Bridge Junction
Hayes & Harlington
Boston Manor
Chiswick
Paddington Branch
Westbourne Park
Paddington
Heathrow Airport
Kew Bridge
Kew Gardens
Hammersmith
Barnes
Mortlake
Richmond
Richmond
River Crane
Twickenham
Richmond Park
Fulham
RIVER THAMES
Putney Bridge
Putney
Wandsworth
River Wandle
Teddington Lock
Teddington
Kingston
Merton
Morden
Hampton Court
Molesey Lock

Coventry City Council	
WHO	
3 8002 01743 044 0	
Askews & Holts	Mar-2011
914.210022	£19.99
VC 23/6/11	

Contents

Introduction

London's Thames

London owes its very existence to the Thames. The river's history goes back to Neolithic times when there is evidence of human occupation on its banks. In those days the winding Thames would have been flanked by marshes watered by tides and tributary rivers. In later years the Romans sailed up the river and established a settlement they called Londinium. The first London Bridge was built by the Romans around AD 50. This wooden bridge and its successors either collapsed, were washed away or burnt down. The first stone London Bridge was built in 1204 and lasted for 600 years. It was the only crossing point for over 500 years until another bridge was built at Westminster.

For centuries the river was London's only highway for trade and people. Kings and queens passed along the river in their royal barges between watermen ferrying people across. By the end of the 18th century, it is estimated that 40,000 watermen worked on the tidal river, but as new bridges were built during the 19th century, their numbers declined.

By this time most of the tidal river between Brentford and Gravesend was lined with wharves busy loading and unloading ships from all over the world. All this congestion on the river bank led to the building of the first London Docks. The first dock was opened in 1802 on the Isle of Dogs, quickly followed by others at Wapping, Blackwall and then the Surrey Docks south of the river at Rotherhithe. By 1886 there were seven separate enclosed dock systems within the Port of London. In 1930, London docks employed 100,000 people but within 50 years they had all closed through labour disputes and deep water containerisation moving to Tilbury. There is still some commercial traffic left on the river today but this is mainly confined to rubbish containers going to landfill sites in Essex. Most of today's boating is for pleasure, with large passenger trip boats passing up and down the river between Hampton Court and Greenwich.

London's Canals

Britain's first navigable canal was built in Manchester in 1761. Before then there was no efficient method of transport to move bulk raw materials and manufactured goods to and from factories and foundries created during the Industrial Revolution. By 1790, most of the industrial areas of the North and Midlands were connected to rivers that in turn led to ports such as Liverpool, Hull and Bristol. Boats carrying produce from the Midlands to London had to undertake an arduous journey by the narrow locked Oxford Canal to Oxford, followed by a long haul along the winding River Thames to the capital. A quicker and more direct route was needed and this was provided by the construction of the Grand Junction Canal, which eventually reached the

Thames at Brentford in 1800. This chopped 60 miles off the previous journey and the broader locks made it possible to accommodate wide barges or for two full length narrow boats to share a lock. The building of the Paddington Arm was followed by the Regent's Canal which, in 1820, created an alternative route to London's Docks. The canal to Paddington followed a level lock-free course in an arc across what are now the north-west London suburbs. As industry sprouted on its banks its workforce needed houses to live in. Villages expanded into towns that later merged to form part of Greater London. The terminus at Paddington became a thriving inland port less than a mile from Marble Arch. The nine-mile-long Regent's Canal begins at Little Venice at Paddington and passes through Regent's Park and Camden on its way to Limehouse where it meets the Thames. Regent's Canal Dock (now Limehouse Marina) was an integral part of the Docklands, handling a wide diversity of cargoes up to the late 1960s. There were canals south of the Thames but these have all been filled in and have almost completely disappeared.

River Lee

This river has a split personality. The natural river is spelled Lea but the navigation is called Lee. The navigation runs from Hertford to the Thames and is joined by the River Stort Navigation near Hoddesdon. It is one of Britain's oldest navigations and there is evidence that Danish Vikings rowed up the river to plunder Hertford. In 1425, an Act of Parliament was passed to improve its navigable status and in 1577, one of the country's earliest pound locks was built at Waltham Abbey. The present navigation was built around 1770 and became busy carrying such commodities as grain, timber, gunpowder, coal, malt and barley. Commercial activity has now ceased but the river's position passing through urban east London has made it an important recreational asset which led to the creation of the Lee Valley Regional Park.

London's Other Waterways

The Thames in London is fed by numerous tributaries. Of these, the Lee is the largest river but other visible waterways include the Brent in west London, the Wandle in south-west London and the Roding in east London. All these rivers (including smaller ones such as the River Crane, Yeading Brook and Beverley Brook) can be followed by footpaths. Several rivers have disappeared underground and have an important role flushing out London's sewage system. Of these the Fleet, Westbourne, Tyburn, Neckinger and Effra are among rivers that were once visible but only had limited navigation. Occasionally these hidden rivers show themselves on the surface – often in surprising places. At other times, their subterranean presence is hinted at by names of streets or even stations.

The aim of this book is not only to show readers the obvious waterside attractions known to visitors from all over the world but to spotlight the often unknown corners that may be surprising even to residents of the capital city.

One of the two bascules that lift to allow a large boat to pass underneath Tower Bridge. Most of today's boating traffic is small enough to pass under the bridge without it being raised.

London's Thames

Travelling on foot or by water, the Thames is accessible to everyone. This was not always the case, as up to the mid-20th century much of the river bank was lined by working wharves, warehouses and docks. In particular, most of the south bank between Wandsworth and Woolwich was largely inaccessible to the public. The north side had its embankments built by Bazalgette in the 19th century and there were views of the river from the bridges.

The big change on the south bank began in 1951 with the Festival of Britain. Old industrial buildings and railway sidings were transformed into the South Bank Exhibition. Most of the exhibits were housed in the Dome of Discovery, which celebrated British post-war achievements in the field of science and industry. A new concert hall called the Royal Festival Hall concentrated on the arts and the slim 250 foot high precariously balanced Skylon amazed everyone. Altogether, the Festival attracted over eight million visitors. Most of the Festival buildings were demolished at the end of 1951 except for the Royal Festival Hall which became the first of many arts-related buildings on the South Bank. The South Bank Centre now includes the Hayward Gallery, the National Film Theatre and the National Theatre, which has three theatres under one roof.

You can follow the South Bank promenade all the way to Tower Bridge and beyond to Bermondsey and Rotherhithe. Its many attractions include the Tate Modern art gallery housed in the old Bankside Power Station, Shakespeare's Globe Theatre, Hay's Galleria, HMS *Belfast* and the London Eye observation wheel built to celebrate the Millennium. Another recent addition to London's south bank is the distinctive City Hall next to Tower Bridge and opposite the Tower of London. Lord Foster's controversial leaning glass building is the home of the Mayor of London and the London Assembly.

London's river that once bustled with ships and barges is now busy with passenger trip boats. Several companies operate passenger boats as far apart as Hampton Court and Greenwich, with a wide variety of routes to choose from. Westminster Pier is the best starting place to experience the river in central London. Many companies offer lunch and dinner cruises or evening parties and it is even possible to hire an original Thames sailing barge.

*Albert Bridge illuminates the Thames
with around 4,000 light bulbs.*

Hampton Court

Main picture Hampton Court Palace by the River Thames. Cardinal Wolsey began building the palace in 1515 and it became the largest house in England. In 1529, Wolsey presented the palace to King Henry VIII as an appeasement to regain Royal pleasure. Henry acquired a fine palace but bestowed little gratitude on Wolsey, who was arrested for treason and died at Leicester en route to London for his probable execution in 1530. The palace's size and splendour made it ideal for a royal residence and five of Henry's wives lived there. Henry made significant additions to the building, including the great hall. More improvements were made by Sir Christopher Wren for William III around 1700.

Below left Balls of mistletoe hanging in this tree by the palace have a sinister appearance in the winter light. Mistletoe was once believed to offer protection from evil and was also a symbol of fertility.

Below right The south facing facade built by Sir Christopher Wren overlooks the formal Privy Gardens. Hampton Court has many other attractions outside the palace and its royal apartments. There are 60 acres of beautiful gardens which include the famous maze and a 230-year-old grape vine which has its own special greenhouse. Beyond the gardens is the 750 acre Home Park, which is home to 300 fallow deer and the setting for the annual flower show.

Bottom The annual flower festival at Hampton Court is now a rival to the Chelsea Flower Show. It is held in July and attracts a large number of visitors from all over the world. A very pleasant way to visit the show is by passenger boat from Westminster, Kew, Kingston or Richmond, thereby avoiding crowded roads and trains. The journey from Westminster can take up to four hours depending on the state of the tide.

Kingston

Main picture Young canoeists under the guidance of an instructor on the river at Kingston. Canoeists need to take care as this is a busy section of the river, with sailing boats, pleasure craft and passenger trip boats all sharing the water.

Below Seven Saxon Kings were crowned at Kingston between AD901 and 978 and their Coronation Stone can be seen outside the Guildhall. For years the stone was used in the market place as a mounting block for horsemen. It was moved to its present position in 1935.

Top middle The first bridge over the river at Kingston was a flimsy wooden structure which was so narrow that traffic could only cross in single file. For many years it was the first crossing above London, which made it strategically important in times of conflict. The present bridge was built in 1828.

Bottom middle Clattern Bridge over the Hogsmill River dates back to the 13th century and possibly derives its name from the sound of horse's hooves clattering over the bridge.

Teddington Lock

Main picture A passenger trip boat leaves Teddington Lock. Teddington has three locks and marks the tidal boundary of the Thames. The barge lock is 650 feet long and is easily the biggest on the entire river. There is also a tiny 50 foot skiff lock but most boats pass through the medium size launch lock. All three locks can clearly be seen behind the passenger boat, which has just left the launch lock.

Top and middle A Tudor pageant at Teddington Lock in June 2009. The pageant was part of many celebrations to mark the 500th anniversary of Henry VIII's coronation in June 1509. A flotilla of traditional shallops and cutters rowed from Tower Bridge to Hampton Court. King Henry and his son Edward can be seen towards the rear of the Royal Shallop *Jubilant*.

Bottom right This elegant footbridge crosses the river between the weir and the lock. It connects Teddington Television Studios, the Landmark Art Centre and two pubs to the Thames towpath.

Twickenham and Ham House

Main picture Marble Hill House was built in 1729 by George II for his mistress Henrietta Howard, Countess of Suffolk, when he was Prince of Wales. This Palladian villa set in 66 acres of riverside parkland became a fashionable meeting place for the literary smart set of that period. A ferry boat carries passengers across the river to Ham House.

Top left An autumnal stroll along the towpath at Ham Lands, an area of woodland near Ham House.

Bottom left The York House Gardens Statues at Twickenham features a group of ladies cavorting around a large fountain representing sea nymphs of Greek mythology. Made in Italian white marble, they were sculptured in the early 19th century at a Rome studio. They can be seen in a garden opposite Eel Pie Island. The island achieved fame during the early 1960s when its hotel provided the venue for blossoming pop groups such as The Rolling Stones and The Who.

Below Ham House, a fine Stuart mansion built in 1610, became a centre for political intrigues during the turbulent 17th century. The house contains many paintings and the formal gardens are famous for their lavender parterres. Since 1948 it has been owned by the National Trust.

Richmond Park

Main picture The Beverley Brook in Richmond Park. This lovely little river was once polluted with badly treated effluent from a sewage works. It has now been completely cleaned and species of fish absent for decades have returned. A footpath follows the river through Wimbledon Common, Richmond Park and Barnes Common. Beverley Brook finally meets the Thames by the boathouses at Putney.

Below The Pen Ponds in Richmond Park were dug in 1746 to resemble natural lakes. Today they are popular with anglers and, in this case, a horse who wanted to cool off on a hot day.

Top middle The Star and Garter Home for disabled servicemen was opened in 1924 by King George V and Queen Mary. It stands on Richmond Hill at the entrance to Richmond Park and has an unrivalled view over the Thames Valley. It is hard to believe that this bucolic scene is so close to bustling Richmond town centre.

Bottom middle Richmond Park covers 2,500 acres and is the largest open space in London. It became a royal hunting park in 1625 when hundreds of deer were introduced and a wall was built around it. It was opened to the public in the mid-18th century. There is a population of over 600 deer in the park today, including these two young fallow deer stags.

Richmond

Main picture A boat passes Richmond's terraced gardens, which rise steeply to Richmond Hill.

Centre left The Thames is fully tidal as far as Richmond footbridge. To maintain adequate water levels for navigation between Richmond and Teddington Lock, the river is kept above half-tide level by means of sluice gates suspended under the footbridge. These work from two hours before high water to two hours afterwards.

Bottom The renowned view of the Thames from Richmond Hill has been an inspiration for artists such as JMW Turner and Sir Joshua Reynolds, who lived nearby. Glover's Island in the middle of the river was named after its owner, Joseph Glover, who was a Thames waterman. In 1898, he put the island up for auction, threatening to sell it to a soap company to use as an advertising hoarding. However, a local resident bought the island and gave it to Richmond Council, thereby preserving the unspoilt view we see today.

Centre right The five-arched Richmond Bridge was built in 1777, replacing an earlier horse ferry. It was built in Portland stone and was the subject of a painting by Turner in 1808. Richmond's riverside has a floating restaurant, a pier for passenger trip boats and a stepped terrace surrounded by pubs and restaurants. On a summer weekend, thousands of visitors turn the town into a busy inland resort. Richmond has a green with a cricket pitch surrounded by 18th century houses. It also has a popular theatre and the remains of a royal palace.

Kew Gardens

Main picture The magnificent Palm House is home to a collection of plants from tropical rainforests. It was built in 1848 by Decimus Burton who also designed the even larger Temperate House. Other notable buildings in the gardens include Kew Palace and the Princess of Wales Conservatory, where you can walk through ten climatic zones.

Top The treetop walkway was opened in May 2008. It is 656 feet long and 60 feet high and gives the visitor a 'bird's eye' view of the Temperate House and surrounding area.

Bottom left Kew Gardens looks really wonderful in springtime when thousands of daffodils and other spring bulbs come into flower.

Below right Kew's Chinese Pagoda was built in 1762 and once had 80 gold plated dragons. These were taken away when the wooden supports rotted away. When it was built, it was the tallest reconstruction of a Chinese pagoda in Europe. In 1843, Decimus Burton wanted to restore it to its former glory but the estimated price of over £4,000 was too much to pay. The Pagoda is 163 feet high, has 253 steps to the top, but at present is closed to the public.

Kew Bridge Steam Museum

Main picture The Steam Hall at Kew Bridge Steam Museum. The machine painted green is the Hathorn Davey Triple Expansion Engine built at Leeds in 1910. It was used in a pumping station at Newmarket.

Below The Kew Bridge Steam Museum's 200-foot-high tower is a landmark beside the Thames. The museum is open to the public throughout the year.

Top The Waddon Engine was built in 1910 by James Simpson & Co in Pimlico for the Waddon Pumping Station at Croydon. It closed down in 1982 after seventy years of service.

Bottom right The beam of the Grand Junction 90 Inch Engine, which is the world's largest working beam engine. It was built in 1846 at the Copperhouse Foundry at Hayle in Cornwall.

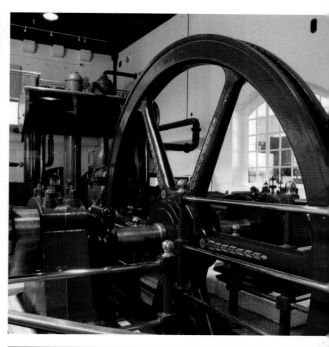

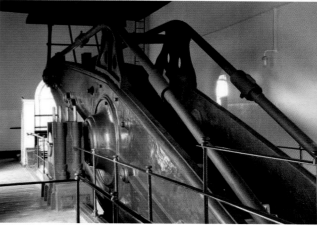

Chiswick and Mortlake

Main picture The promenade at Strand-on-the-Green is popular, especially on summer evenings when its waterside pubs and footpath attract many visitors. It began as a fishing village and some of its surviving waterside cottages were home to fishermen and boatmen's families. In later years general trading took place at Strand-on-the Green until the opening of the Grand Junction Canal diverted traffic to Brentford. In 1966, the Beatles filmed scenes here for their movie *Help!* During the early part of the 20th century, Strand-on-the Green became a fashionable place to live and it has remained largely undeveloped with many original Georgian houses.

Bottom Barnes Railway Bridge attracts the nation's television spotlight once a year when it is the last bridge the University crews negotiate before the end of the Boat Race. It was built in 1891 and has a footbridge that connects Dukes Meadows in Chiswick to Mortlake High Street. The Bull's Head pub, by the river at Mortlake, is renowned as a centre for mainstream and modern jazz. Most of the top British jazz artists (such as Humphrey Lyttelton) have played here and many of them have become regular performers at the pub.

Below right Chiswick House was built in the neo-Palladian style for Lord Burlington in 1728. It became a showcase for the arts rather than a residence. There is an extensive park with a lake and ornamental bridge. Over the years it has been a mental institution and for a short time housed an exotic zoo. It is now owned by English Heritage and is open to the public.

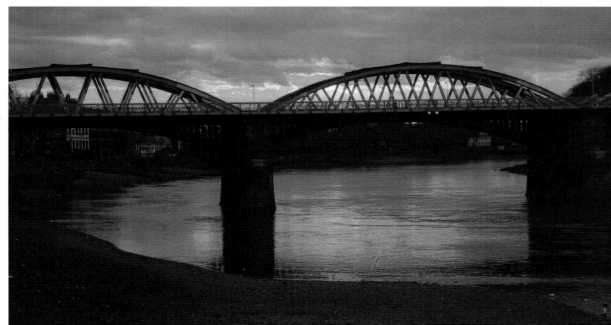

Hammersmith

Main picture Hammersmith Bridge was designed by Victorian engineer Sir Joseph Bazalgette in 1887, replacing an earlier suspension bridge by William Tierney Clarke. The old bridge was declared unsafe after 12,000 people crowded on to it to watch the Boat Race in 1870. Hammersmith Bridge has survived being a target for terrorist bombs on two occasions. William Morris, founder of the Arts and Crafts movement, lived in nearby Kelmscott House between 1878 until his death in 1896. The house is now a museum dedicated to his memory.

Below A number of riverside pubs make Hammersmith a meeting place for (mostly) young people on Boat Race Day. Author AP Herbert, who lived in Hammersmith terrace, featured the 17th century Dove pub (nearby) in his book *The Water Gypsies*, renamed *The Pigeon*.

London Wetland Centre

Main picture Located by the river at Barnes, the London Wetland Centre is home to a wide variety of native and migrating birds. It was created on a site of disused reservoirs for the Wildfowl and Wetlands Trust by its founder Sir Peter Scott. During the summer months, parts of the Wetland Centre are ablaze with wildflowers. Strategically positioned hides make the site popular with serious bird watchers, while a maze of walks followed by a visit to the cafe and shop make it equally popular with family visitors. The London Wetland Centre was recognised as a Site of Special Scientific Interest in 2002.

Below Parts of the grazing marsh covered with a carpet of wild daisies in the springtime.

Bottom left The Egyptian Goose was introduced to Britain about 300 years ago. Breeding colonies were established in Norfolk in the 19th century and even today 90% of the population still remains in that county.

Bottom right The Black-necked Swan is a native of southern South America. They are successfully breeding at the Wetland Centre.

Putney and Fulham

Main picture The end of the Head of the River race at Putney. The race involves 3,780 competitors (420 crews of eight rowers plus a cox) and is rowed over four and a quarter miles between Mortlake and Putney. This is in the opposite direction to the University Boat Race, which usually takes place a week later towards the end of March. Crews leave at ten second intervals to avoid bunching. The women's race over the same distance takes place on an earlier date to the men's.

Below Fulham Palace was the home of the Bishops of London from the 11th century to 1975. The palace, which has an exhibition gallery, is now open to the public. The palace grounds and the neighbouring Bishop's Park have riverside walks and flower gardens.

Above right Craven Cottage, home to Fulham Football Club, is attractively situated on the north bank of the Thames. The statue to the late Johnny Haynes was erected in 2008 at the entrance to the ground. Haynes was Fulham's most famous player from 1950 to 1970 during which time he won 56 caps for England.

Below right This memorial to Steve Fairburn, who founded the Head of the River race in 1926, can be seen by the towpath exactly one mile from the start of the Boat Race at Putney.

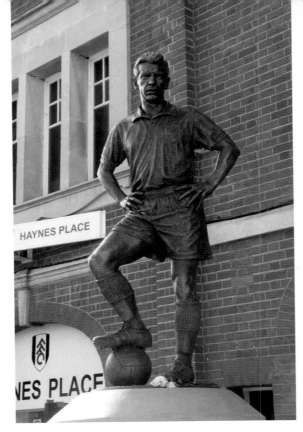

Chelsea

Main picture View from Battersea Bridge of the permanent houseboat moorings at Cheyne Walk in front of Lots Road Power station. The power station opened in 1904 to provide power for London's underground railway and continued in operation until 2002. The site is central to a huge development to create a new waterside village with riverside walks that will connect to Chelsea Creek, Chelsea Harbour and Imperial Wharf. The tall building in the background is the Belvedere Tower, which marks the entrance to Chelsea Harbour. The artist James McNeil Whistler painted this scene several times. His 'Nocturne in Black and Gold: The Falling Rocket' was described by Ruskin as 'flinging a pot of paint in the public's face'. Whistler sued Ruskin for libel and was awarded just a farthing in damages. A statue to Whistler stands in a small garden at the north end of Battersea Bridge.

Below A miscellany of expensive boats moored in Chelsea Harbour. The marina is overlooked by hotels, apartments and a smart design centre.

Above right The Cremorne Gates once formed the entrance to Cremorne Pleasure Gardens, which stretched along the north side of the river at Chelsea. These fashionable gardens became a popular meeting place between 1840 and 1877, when complaints about its notoriety forced it to close down. The gardens, which were illuminated at night by gas lamps, had firework displays, dancing and balloon ascents. In 1864, Madame Genevieve Young known as the 'Female Blondini' crossed the Thames between Battersea and Cremorne Gardens on a tightrope.

Battersea

Main picture Albert Bridge is one of the most striking bridges in central London, particularly at night when it is illuminated by thousands of bulbs. A sign at either side of the bridge orders marching troops to break step when crossing the bridge. It was built in 1871 but structural defects almost led to its permanent closure in the mid 1970s.

Left The Peace Pagoda by the river in Battersea Park was a gift to London in 1985 from the Japanese Order of Buddhists. Battersea Park was opened in 1858 to provide 'healthy recreation for the lower orders'. The park has a subtropical garden and a beautiful lake with a fine sculpture by Barbara Hepworth. In 1951, the park was part of the Festival of Britain celebrations and its fun fair remained there until the end of the decade.

Bottom left The ancient riverside church of St Mary's, Battersea, has been engulfed by modern buildings. This was a favourite place for the artist JMW Turner, who regularly painted from here. William Blake was married here in 1782 and has a window dedicated to his memory. The American traitor Benedict Arnold is buried in the crypt along with other members of his family.

Below Albert Bridge notice for troops.

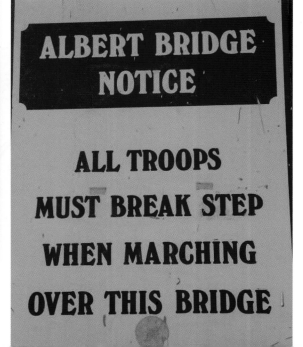

ALBERT BRIDGE NOTICE

ALL TROOPS MUST BREAK STEP WHEN MARCHING OVER THIS BRIDGE

Chelsea Reach

Main picture The silhouetted outline of Battersea Power Station. Built by Sir Giles Gilbert Scott in 1937, the power station generated electricity for London until its closure in 1983. Since then it has remained unused but the future for this iconic riverside landmark may be as the centre of a leisure, conference and housing complex.

Top The Chelsea Physic Garden was founded by the Society of Apothecaries in 1673 so that their apprentices could grow and learn about medicinal plants. In 1712, the garden was bought by Doctor Hans Sloane who appointed botanist Philip Miller as head gardener. The garden became world famous during Miller's fifty-year tenure when he wrote his *Dictionary of Gardening*, which became a standard reference work. The garden, which still promotes education and scientific research, is London's oldest botanical garden and is next to the Chelsea Embankment.

Bottom The Royal Hospital, designed by Sir Christopher Wren, was opened in 1690 to care for army veterans. The old soldiers wear a distinctive scarlet uniform and are affectionately known as 'Chelsea Pensioners'. The Hospital is built around three courtyards with a golden statue of founder Charles II in the centre of the main square. In 1852, the Duke of Wellington lay in state here for seven days during which time two people died in the crush to view the great man's coffin. The Chelsea Flower Show takes place in the Hospital grounds every year.

Vauxhall

Main picture An approaching storm at Vauxhall Bridge. The present bridge was built in 1906, replacing an earlier cast iron toll bridge that had become unstable. Statues on the abutments at each side of the bridge commemorate women's achievements in arts and science; for example, the woman holding a vase represents pottery.

Centre top Vauxhall City Farm was opened in 1977 on a patch of derelict land at the edge of Spring Gardens. It is run by a team of dedicated volunteers and contains a wide variety of farm animals plus a few exotic species like the baby alpaca in the photograph. Spring Gardens is the site of the famous Vauxhall Pleasure Gardens, which opened in 1660.

In 1749 a rehearsal for Handel's Fireworks Music drew 12,000 spectators. Like Cremorne Gardens it featured music, fireworks, fountains and balloon ascents. It eventually closed down in 1859 when the owners declared themselves bankrupt.

Centre bottom Figure with vase – see above.

Right The Tate Gallery, now renamed Tate Britain, was founded in 1897 by the sugar magnate Sir Henry Tate. It was built on the site of the former Millbank prison. Tate Britain contains a large collection of British art from 1500 onwards. A special collection of paintings by JMW Turner can be seen in the Clore Gallery.

Westminster

Main picture Westminster Bridge and the Houses of Parliament. The Palace of Westminster was a royal residence until 1512 after which it became parliament: 'a place to speak'. After a disastrous fire in 1834, the medieval building was replaced by the present building designed and built by Sir Charles Barry and Augustus Pugin. It was completed in 1847 and ever since has remained the seat of government. The first Westminster Bridge opened in 1750 but suffered from subsidence and was replaced in 1862 by the present structure.

Below Westminster view from Lambeth Bridge.

Right One of the faces of Big Ben, Britain's most famous clock. It is named after the largest bell inside the 320-foot-high clock tower. This face has a Latin inscription that translates, 'O Lord save our Queen Victoria the First'. The time is regulated by adding or taking away an old penny, which makes the difference of four fifths of a second. The name originated after a three hour debate in the chamber of the House of Commons on what to call the bell. Sir Benjamin Hall, who was a large man, got up to speak and a heckler shouted, 'Why not call it Big Ben and be done with it?' The name stuck!

Victoria Embankment

Main picture The London Marathon passes along the Victoria Embankment. This annual springtime event attracts huge crowds along its 26 mile course starting in south-east London, crossing Tower Bridge into Docklands and finishing at Westminster. The Victoria Embankment was built by the great Victorian engineer Sir Joseph Bazalgette in 1868. The embankments not only protect London's riverside from flooding at high tide but also conceal Bazalgette's underground sewage system. A memorial plaque can be seen on the embankment wall at the bottom left of the photograph.

Top left The Battle of Britain memorial on the Victoria Embankment commemorates all the people, both military and civilian, who were killed during the Battle of Britain in 1940. It features a series of relief sculptures in bronze and was opened by the Prince of Wales in 2005.

Bottom left The Victoria Embankment Gardens provide a green oasis where office workers can sit, eat their lunch and enjoy the peaceful surroundings. The digging of the District Underground Railway supplied the subsoil for the gardens, topped by soil from Barking Creek. The gardens contain a mixture of deciduous trees and shrubs with summer bedding plants. The statue to the right of the photograph is to the memory of the Victorian composer Sir Arthur Sullivan (1842 – 1900) who achieved fame with his light operas in collaboration with librettist WS Gilbert. The nearby Savoy Theatre was originally built by Richard D'Oyly Carte to perform Gilbert & Sullivan operettas.

South Bank

Main picture An outdoor cafe outside the Festival Hall. It was the 1951 Festival of Britain that first put the spotlight on this part of the river. The centre-piece of the Festival was the Festival Hall, which was later joined by the National Film Theatre, the Hayward Gallery and the National Theatre to form the South Bank Arts Centre. The promenade between Westminster Bridge and Waterloo Bridge is one of the liveliest places in London, with live music, living statues, book stalls, shops, cafes and restaurants.

Top right Since the year 2000 the South Bank has been dominated by the London Eye observation wheel. It gives wonderful views of London and has 32 revolving capsules which represent the 32 London boroughs. Each rotation takes about 30 minutes and the wheel attracts four million visitors each year.

Right Playing the blues! Street musicians and living statues are commonplace on the South Bank promenade.

Below right Watch This Space is the National Theatre's annual summer outdoor festival of music and theatre on the South Bank.

Waterloo Bridge

Main picture A passenger trip boat leaves the Festival Pier in front of Waterloo Bridge. This is one of many that operate from piers in central London. Sir Giles Gilbert Scott's Waterloo Bridge was built in 1945, replacing an earlier one by John Rennie. Somerset House is in the background behind the bridge. The ship moored next to the bridge is the TS *Queen Mary* which was once a cruising ship on the River Clyde and the Western Isles. It is now a bar and can be hired for private parties.

Bottom The ice rink at Somerset House is very popular with skaters for a few weeks before and after Christmas. This magnificent building was originally on the riverside with an archway to accommodate entry for the Royal Barge. Bazalgette's embankment separated the house from the river's edge in 1870. Somerset House is the home of the Courtauld Gallery but also stages exhibitions, live music and cinema. The courtyard features 55 fountains during the months when it isn't an ice rink. Somerset House can be seen on the north bank of the Thames next to Waterloo Bridge.

Right top London's city skyline underlined by Waterloo Bridge. Notable buildings include St Paul's Cathedral, The NatWest Tower and 30 St Mary Axe popularly known as 'The Gherkin' designed by Sir Norman Foster.

Bankside

Main picture   A bird's eye view of Bankside from the top of St Paul's Cathedral. In Tudor times, Bankside was a centre for brothels, bear baiting and playhouses like the Globe. The reconstructed Shakespeare's Globe Theatre can be seen to the left of the Tate Gallery. They are connected to St Paul's and the north bank by the Millennium footbridge.

Top left   The Millennium footbridge opened in June 2000 but closed three days later due to lateral vibration when thousands of visitors caused the bridge to wobble. Modifications took almost two years before the bridge was deemed to be safe. From the bridge there are superb views of the river and St Paul's Cathedral.

Bottom right   A plaque on the wall of Cardinal's Wharf states 'Here lived Sir Christopher Wren during the building of St Paul's Cathedral'. However, it has been disputed that Wren lived there at all. The house can be seen sandwiched between the Tate Modern and Globe Theatre.

Left bottom   The Tate Modern Art Gallery located in the old Bankside Power Station houses the nation's 20th century collection of modern art. A succession of spectacular large-scale displays have been held in the turbine hall. Entry to the gallery is free except for major exhibitions.

London Bridge

Main picture Thames sailing barges moored at London Bridge City Pier. Built in 1176, the Old London Bridge had nineteen stone arches of various widths and its entire length supported a street of timber-framed houses. The narrow arches slowed down the river's flow to such an extent that in some severe winters the Thames froze over upstream, leading to Frost Fairs on the ice. Downstream the force of water scoured the bed of the river, enabling large ships to use the port. This area is still called the Pool of London. A grisly feature of the old bridge was the display of heads, once attached to traitors and criminals, on the Drawbridge Gate. In 1577, the Drawbridge Gate was replaced by the elaborate timber-framed Nonsuch House, which was shipped from Holland. The Old London Bridge remained as the only crossing place in central London until Westminster Bridge was built in 1739. The present bridge that opened in 1973 replaced an earlier structure built by John Rennie in 1831, which was subsequently sold to an American and moved piece by piece to a lake in Arizona.

Centre top This wall plaque near London Bridge commemorates the visit to London's biggest brewery by the Austrian General Haynau in 1850. He was nicknamed 'General Hyena' because of his brutal suppression of Italian and Hungarian revolutionaries in 1848. Brewery draymen attacked the general and dragged him along the street by his moustache. He was eventually rescued by police.

Centre bottom Plaque commemorating 'The Great Fire of Tooley Street'.

Right Hay's Galleria was once part of Hay's Wharf famous for its fleet of tea clippers bringing tea from India. Hay's Wharf was also known as The Larder of London because of the imported dairy produce mostly from New Zealand. It was the site of 'The Great Fire of Tooley Street' in 1861 (see photo of plaque), which led to the founding of the London Fire Brigade. Today, Hay's Galleria is a shopping arcade with bars and restaurants under a covered atrium. David Kemp's kinetic sculpture 'The Navigators' forms a centrepiece to the building.

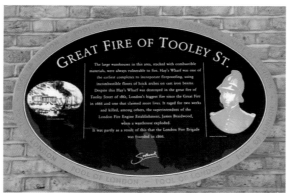

Tower of London

Main picture and below Built in the reign of William the Conqueror, the Tower is universally renowned as one of Britain's most historic buildings. Over the centuries it has served many purposes – as a royal palace, a prison, armoury, royal mint and a safe storage place for the Crown Jewels. Tower Green was the place of execution for Anne Boleyn, Catherine Howard, Lady Jane Grey and many others who displeased the Tudor monarchs. Many notables would have made their last journeys to the Tower by river, entering through Traitor's Gate. In 1934, 1,500 barge-loads of sand were deposited on the Tower foreshore to create a beach for the children of the East End. Tower Beach was a huge attraction for local families despite the limited time it could be opened because of the tides. It finally closed in 1971 because of rising pollution levels. The Tower remains a busy tourist centre popular with visitors from all over the world who arrive by boat at Tower Pier.

Below A statue of the Emperor Trajan stands next to the remaining section of Roman City Wall outside Tower Hill underground station.

Tower Bridge

Main picture One of the world's most famous bridges and an iconic symbol of London. It was built in 1894 at a time when the Pool of London was still a busy port and the bridge's bascules were raised many times a day to allow large ships to pass through. The original hydraulic lifting machinery has been replaced by electric. Much of the old machinery has been preserved and can be seen as part of the Tower Bridge Exhibition. The upper part of the bridge has a walkway that became the haunt of robbers and prostitutes and which led to its eventual closure. It has now reopened and is part of the exhibition where visitors can enjoy spectacular views of the river and surrounding area.

Below London's City Hall stands on the south bank next to Tower Bridge and opposite the Tower of London. Designed by Norman Foster and opened in July 2002, this leaning glass building is in complete contrast to the historical structures in its vicinity. It is the workplace of the London Assembly and the Mayor of London.

Bottom Tower Bridge closing behind a Thames Sailing Barge. This barge is one of about 30 barges still licensed to sail, although others are being restored. In 1907 there were 2,090 registered sailing barges working on the coast around the Thames estuary carrying various cargoes into the capital. The barges' flat-bottom hull allowed them to sail up shallow creeks off the coast of Essex and Kent. There is an annual Thames Barge Race on the Thames Estuary that starts and finishes at Gravesend.

Docklands

London has been one of the world's major ports since ancient times. Trade steadily increased over the years until the end of the 18th century, when pressure grew to reorganise the port due to a huge boom in business. This was brought on by imports from overseas and from within Britain where the new canal system brought produce from England's industrial heartland into London.

The main problems were lack of warehouse space, security and time lost by ships waiting for mooring places and for the tide to change. This led to the creation of large, enclosed docks throughout east London with quaysides lined by warehouses with high surrounding walls, and locks to control tidal movement in and out of the river. Most dock workers were employed on a casual basis with a 'call-on' in early morning when hundreds of men would compete to catch the foreman's eye for the few jobs that were available.

By 1886, the Port of London had seven enclosed docks on both sides of the river but by now trade was declining and some of the dock companies were in financial difficulties. By the turn of the century, the Port of London Authority had taken control of the existing dock companies and begun a programme of modernisation. The King George V Dock opened in 1921, completing the Royal group of docks, which in its entirety formed the largest area of enclosed docks in the world. They also handled passengers as their deep water could berth large liners. The Royal Docks remained busy and prosperous until the mid-20th century when containerisation and loss of business to European competitors led to a sharp decline in trade. Cargo handling was transferred to Tilbury where there was deeper water and better technology, and one by one the London docks all closed by the beginning of the 1980s.

The London Docklands Development Corporation was formed to secure regeneration by bringing in new industry and commerce, and creating an attractive environment to encourage people to live and work in the area. Many of the docks, which had degenerated into a wasteland of dereliction, were transformed into new housing and office buildings. The focal point of the new Docklands is the Canary Wharf complex with its towering office buildings visible for miles around. Canary Wharf is connected to the City of London by the Docklands Light Railway, the Jubilee tube line and improved road access. A large underground shopping mall has been created beneath Canary Wharf and there are more shops, restaurants and bars at ground level.

Surrey Quays has similar facilities south of the river on the site of the old Surrey Docks. St Katharine Dock, which is adjacent to Tower Bridge and the Tower of London, has become a major tourist attraction with its marina, pub and shops surrounded by the splendid Ivory House and restored warehouses. London's Dockland (once a closed area to anyone who wasn't actually employed there) is now open to everyone and has taken on a new lease of life.

A sailing boat on the main West India Dock with a backdrop of Canary Wharf. The boat is heading for the lock, which is the only connection between the docks of the Isle of Dogs and the Thames.

Wapping

Main picture St Katharine Dock was built by Thomas Telford in 1828. It lies on the river's north bank very close to Tower Bridge and the Tower of London. A large basin, now used as a marina, leads to two smaller docks. They are surrounded by a series of splendid old buildings that include the Ivory House (pictured). Other original buildings were badly damaged during the Second World War and those parts of the dock have been redeveloped for residential purposes. In its commercial heyday, St Katharine Dock specialised in handling valuable imported cargoes.

Below left A memorial to the civilians of East London who were killed in the Blitz can be seen in the riverside Hermitage Memorial Gardens at Wapping. The peace dove sculpture is by Wendy Taylor.

Bottom left Wapping Old Stairs by the Town of Ramsgate pub was the place where convicts boarded ships that took them to the colonies.

Below The Town of Ramsgate pub in Wapping. This is reputed to be the site of Execution Dock, where pirates, thieves and other assorted villains were strung up before the public and left to decay. Other riverside inns like the Captain Kidd and The Prospect of Whitby also claim to be the site of Execution Dock. This is good for business and may have some truth as, over the years, the site could have moved along the river.

Limehouse

Main picture Cruise ship *Silver Wind* at Limehouse Reach. *Silver Wind* was built in 1995 and carries around 300 passengers and 200 crew. She specialises in world-wide luxury cruises.

Top right A crowded trip boat approaches the Isle of Dogs on a fine winter's day. This view of the river looking towards Limehouse and the City of London is from the terrace above Canary Wharf Pier. Early in the 19th century, Limehouse became known as 'Chinatown' and was the home for a large population of Chinese immigrants.

Bottom right Charles Dickens brilliantly describes Limehouse in his novel *Our Mutual Friend*. His pub, The Six Jolly Fellowship Porters, was probably The Grapes in Narrow Street, here seen from the river squeezed between fashionable residences. Many old waterside properties now converted to expensive apartments are in demand for their extensive riverside views. Away from the river, rundown slum dwellings left behind when the working docks closed have been replaced by modern housing.

Canary Wharf

Main picture A view of Canary Wharf from Ratcliffe Cross Stairs at Limehouse. Two Elizabethan explorers, Sir Hugh Willoughby (in 1553) and Martin Frobisher (in 1576), set sail from this point to search for the North-East and North-West Passages through frozen Arctic waters. Canary Wharf has become a major publishing and financial centre and contains London's three tallest buildings. At 771 feet No 1 Canada Square is Britain's highest building.

Below left Canary Wharf from South Quay at West India Dock which was the first of the enclosed London Docks built in 1802. West India Docks were built by William Jessop and John Rennie who were also responsible for many of Britain's canals

still in use today. At first the docks dealt solely with produce from the West Indies and its warehouses contained vast quantities of sugar and molasses.

Bottom left The Blue Lifting Bridge allows boats to enter the West India Docks and Canary Wharf from the Thames. When large cargo vessels arrived at the dock it often took up to half an hour to manoeuvre them past the bridge and into the lock, causing long traffic queues.

Below This modern suspension footbridge crosses a section of the South Dock to the Canary Wharf shopping centre. Canary Wharf has over 200 shops, bars, restaurants and cafés in three underground arcades.

Isle of Dogs

Main picture Young sailors under instruction from the Docklands Sailing and Water Sports centre at Millwall Dock. This dock was once dominated by a huge flour mill, which was a major local employer for over 100 years until its closure in 1982. It was demolished in 1984 and replaced by a large printing works.

Below Grazing llamas on the extensive pasture at Mudchute Farm on the Isle of Dogs. More domestic breeds such as pigs, sheep, cows, ducks and chickens can be seen on what is Europe's largest urban farm. Mudchute also has a riding centre and strips of woodland for wild birds.

Bottom left The domed rotunda entrance to the Greenwich Foot Tunnel at Island Gardens. The tunnel was opened in 1902, giving workers living in Greenwich access to the docks on the Isle of Dogs.

Bottom right An 1895 view of Docklands on a Victorian board game called 'A Race Through London'. Note the long defunct Grand Surrey Canal which, at that time was still a working waterway (courtesy of Gunnersbury Park Museum).

Rotherhithe

Main picture The Lavender Pumphouse was built in 1930 to regulate the water level in the Surrey Commercial Docks. It is now the Rotherhithe Heritage Museum incorporating the Lavender Pond and Nature Park.

Top left The Brunel Museum at Rotherhithe commemorates the Thames Tunnel, which was the world's first tunnel under a navigable waterway. It took eighteen years to build and was completed in 1843. It was built as a pedestrian tunnel, which then became part of London's Underground system. For a while after it opened, Marc Brunel held elaborate banquets inside the tunnel to impress investors. The museum is housed in an engine house that once kept the tunnel dry.

Bottom left A pond in the Russia Dock Woodland ecological park. Russia Dock was the central basin in the Surrey Docks complex. After closure it lay derelict for a while before being filled in and planted with woodland. The extent of this dense forested area can be best viewed from the top of nearby Stave Hill, an artificial mound giving wide views across Docklands and the City of London.

Below The statue of Doctor Salter at Cherry Garden Pier. Doctor Salter was a benevolent local figure who worked hard for the poor and became MP for Bermondsey. The statue shows him waving to his young daughter Joyce who is depicted by the nearby sea wall with her pet cat. Joyce tragically died of scarlet fever while still a child.

Surrey Docks

Main picture A large crane, some mooring bollards and anchors are all reminders of how busy Durand's Wharf was in its commercial heyday. The area has been transformed into a pleasant park with spectacular views across the water to Canary Wharf. There is a proposal to build a cycling and pedestrian bridge over the Thames to connect Durand's Wharf to the Canary Wharf centre.

Top left The Albion Channel which connects Canada Water with Surrey Water is now lined with modern housing. The Surrey Docks were once the world's biggest timber importers from Scandinavian countries but most of the timber wharves were destroyed by enemy bombing in 1940. Greenland Dock, which finally closed as a commercial enterprise in 1970, is now a marina and Surrey Quays is one of London's biggest shopping areas.

Bottom left 'Look out for the fox'. These statues of goats can be seen outside the Surrey Docks Farm. The farm was founded in 1975 on derelict ground near the entrance to Greenland Dock. It moved to its present location at South Wharf in 1986 on the site of a former shipyard.

Below The Grand Surrey Canal opened from the Thames at Greenland Dock in 1807. Initially, there was an ambitious scheme for it to connect to the sea at Portsmouth, but the canal only got as far as Camberwell, where it joined the Croydon Canal. The canal was partially abandoned and went into decline in the 1940s. A short section at Greenland Dock remained in business until 1971. Since then the canal has been filled in and built over.

Greenwich

Main picture The Old Royal Naval College was designed by Christopher Wren and stands on the site of the Tudor Palace of Placentia. Originally used as a hospital for sick seamen, it closed in 1869 and reopened four years later as the Royal Naval College, dedicated to the training of naval officers. The buildings have now become part of the University of Greenwich and the Trinity College of Music. The Chapel and the Painted Hall are both open to the public.

Top left The magnificent ceiling of the Painted Hall is lavishly decorated with paintings by James Thornhill that took him eighteen years to complete. The hall was where, in January 1806, Admiral Nelson lay in state after his death at the Battle of Trafalgar before he was buried in St Paul's Cathedral.

Bottom left The tea clipper *Cutty Sark* stands in a dry dock near Greenwich Pier. The boat, which was built in 1869, carried tea from India and China. It has stood in Greenwich as a maritime museum since 1954. Badly damaged by fire in 2007, it is at the time of writing being completely restored.

Below Greenwich Pier on a busy summer's day. Passenger boats operate between Greenwich and Westminster on a daily service throughout the year.

Greenwich Park

Main picture The view of the Greenwich World Heritage Site from the hilltop in Greenwich Park. The white building in the centre of the view is the Queen's House. It was designed by Inigo Jones and completed in 1635 by King James I for his wife Anne of Denmark. It is now part of the National Maritime Museum.

Right Visitors stand on the Meridian Line at the Royal Observatory in Greenwich Park. This is very popular with tourists, who like to be photographed with one foot in the eastern hemisphere and the other in the west. The Prime Meridian marks zero degrees longitude.

Below The Royal Observatory was built in 1675 by Christopher Wren for Charles II. The first Astronomer Royal was John Flamsteed, whose task was to record the motions of the heavens and fix the place of stars to perfect the art of navigation. It is now a museum of astronomy and timekeeping.

The Millennium Dome

The Dome was originally built to celebrate the Millennium but for a while afterwards its future was uncertain. Now renamed the O2 Arena, it has become one of London's major entertainment centres. The O2 Arena stages concerts and sporting events with a 20,000 capacity. The Dome also has a smaller stage, an eleven screen cinema complex and several restaurants and bars. It will be the venue for gymnastics and basketball at the 2012 London Olympics.

Royal Victoria Dock

Main picture The Royal Victoria Dock opened in 1855 and was the first dock to be built for large steam ships and the first to have direct rail links to the quayside. The soil excavated in building the dock was carried up the river and used to make Battersea Park, which opened in 1858. Royal Victoria Dock is now the site of ExCeL, London's biggest exhibition centre, covering over 100 acres. Every January, ExCeL is host to the London International Boat Show.

Left One of the huge redundant cranes that still line the Royal Victoria Dock. The Royal Docks, with their greater capacity and trans-shipment links remained successful, specialising in handling bulk grain until the 1960s. Spillers Millennium Mills, one of the largest mill buildings ever built in London, can be seen opposite ExCeL. Containerisation and loss of business to European neighbours caused the docks to decline, leading to their eventual closure in 1981.

Below Massed start for the ladies' swimming event at the London Triathlon, held in the Royal Victoria Dock. The Triathlon involves cycling and running as well as swimming and in 2009 it attracted over 13,000 entrants.

Royal Albert Dock

Main picture The Royal Albert Dock opened in 1880 and was one of the last docks to built in London's Dockland. It was almost a mile in length and had three miles of quayside. The group was completed by the construction of the King George V Dock that opened in 1921, giving the Royal Docks a combination of 250 acres. The Royal Albert, which was the first London dock to be lit by electricity, was heavily bombed during the Second World War. It is now the home of the Dockland Regatta.

Below The University of East London is on the north bank of the Royal Albert Dock. The university was opened on this site in the year 2000. It faces across the dock to London City Airport, which lies between the Royal Albert and King George V docks.

Bottom The Sir Steve Redgrave Bridge at the head of the Royal Albert Dock. It seems appropriate that as London is hosting the 2012 Olympic Games a Dockland's bridge should be named after Britain's five-times Olympic gold medal rowing champion.

Silvertown

Main picture This mural on a wall beside St Mark's Church depicts a local street in the heyday of the Royal Docks. Today, Silvertown is dominated by the huge Tate & Lyle sugar factory which has been here since 1880. In January 1917, 50 tons of TNT exploded in a Silvertown chemical works, killing 73 people and devastating the surrounding area.

Below The Brick Lane Music Hall has found a permanent home at the former St Mark's Church at Silvertown. The music hall is the brainchild of comedian Vincent Hayes, who began it in 1992 at a disused brewery in Brick Lane, Whitechapel. St Mark's Church was built in 1861 but was badly damaged by fire in 1981. After it was deconsecrated, the building was carefully restored and then remained empty before becoming the new home of the music hall.

The Thames Barrier

Main picture The Thames Barrier viewed at low tide from the north bank at Thames Barrier Park. In January 1953, a combination of winter gales, high spring tides and a deep area of low pressure caused a huge storm surge in the Thames estuary. Canvey Island on the estuary near Southend was almost submerged and 58 lives were lost. This disaster led to the construction of the Thames Barrier at Woolwich to protect London from flooding. A series of ten rotating gates set on piers fixed to the bed of the river become operational when the river rises to a potentially dangerous level.

Below The Barrier opened in 1984. In January 2003, bad weather forced it to close on 13 consecutive tides.

Woolwich Arsenal

Main picture The Woolwich Ferry opened in 1889 and still operates free of charge. Two boats work every day of the year except Christmas Day and New Year's Day while a third boat is held in reserve. The boats do not run in thick foggy weather. On those occasions pedestrians can cross the river by the foot tunnel.

Below The Old Royal Military Academy stands on the site of a Tudor house called Tower Place. The present building was built in 1720 and became the Royal Military Academy in 1741. In 1806 it became part of the Royal Laboratory and in the 20th century was used as an officer's mess. The entrance to the Greenwich Heritage Centre can be seen on the right of the photograph.

Bottom left The Royal Arsenal Gatehouse, known as the Beresford Gate. This 19th century gatehouse was the main entrance to the Arsenal site.

Bottom right Firepower is the Royal Artillery Museum, which tells the story of the two and a half million men and women who were part of the Royal Artillery and their role in the history of the British Army. They were known as the 'Gunners'. In 1886, workers at the nearby Dial Square gun machining factory formed a football team, which later became Woolwich Arsenal Football Club. In 1913, they moved to Highbury in North London and became the Arsenal, forever known as the 'Gunners'.

London's Canals

There are three canals in London. The Regent's Canal connects the Thames at Limehouse to Little Venice at Paddington, and then the Paddington Arm continues through north-west London to Bulls Bridge near Southall. Finally the Grand Union main line leaves the Thames at Brentford and passes Bulls Bridge on its journey to Birmingham and the north. For the purposes of this book we end at Denham on London's western fringe.

The urban canal towpath was originally designed for the use of working boat horses and not as a thoroughfare for pedestrians. In city areas, access to the canals was often severely restricted and there were even penalties for trespass. When commercial carrying went into decline so did the condition of the city's towpaths and their fencing. The canals often became a play-ground for children who could squeeze through broken down fences. Consequently, the occasional drowning led to inevitable calls to close the canal and fill it in. Fortunately for us today this didn't happen and now the urban canal towpaths are open to everyone and have become recreational assets. All the London canal towpaths have unrestricted access and in some cases have become part of acknowledged long-distance footpaths such as the Grand Union Canal walk from London to Birmingham.

Change is equally apparent with the factories that once relied on the canal for transport. Many of them have gone or have been replaced by anonymous industrial units or housing estates that reflect the past, with names like the Grand Union Village at Northolt. The warehouses of the once bustling depot at Brentford have been replaced by modern apartments and a hotel. At Limehouse the old Regent's Canal Dock is now Limehouse Marina, which is surrounded by new housing. The biggest change of all is the huge development at Paddington. Now called Paddington Waterside it has new offices, residential, leisure and retail outlets built on the former Paddington Basin that had become completely run down and shut off from the public gaze. At nearby Little Venice, visitors to London can take a passenger trip boat along the Regent's Canal to the London Zoo, while colourful Camden Lock has a large market which has become a magnet for tourists. There are several passenger boats operating between Camden Lock and Little Venice.

All of London's surviving canals are north of the Thames. South London canals such as the Grand Surrey and the Croydon Canal became derelict and have been filled in. There were ambitious plans for the Grand Surrey to connect the Thames to Portsmouth but it didn't get any further than Camberwell. Other lost canals such as the Grosvenor Canal and Kensington Canal were no more than short navigable creeks off the Thames. The terminal basin of the Grosvenor Canal is now covered by Victoria Station and the terminus for the Kensington Canal became the station at Olympia.

A canal boat passes under Hampstead Road at Camden Lock.

The Grand Union Main line – Denham Deep Lock

Main picture Denham Deep Lock has a surprisingly remote setting despite the fact it is less than half a mile from the end of the M40 motorway. Being located by the Denham Country Park, it is a good place for walkers, who can stroll by the River Colne as well as the canal towpath. An excellent tea garden in the lock-house is an added attraction.

Below The River Colne flows past Denham Court Mansion and the Buckinghamshire Golf Club.

This lovely place is just a few minutes' walk from the canal through the woodland of Denham Country Park.

Bottom Winter cruising at Denham Deep Lock. Icy conditions like this can be fun for today's pleasure boaters but in the days of the working boatmen a frozen canal often meant loss of earnings if they were unable to deliver their cargoes on time.

Cowley Lock

Main picture Cowley Lock, with its nearby pub and restaurant, is a popular stopping place for boaters. The lock marks the end (or beginning) of a 27-mile lock-free pound that stretches as far as Camden Lock and includes the Slough Arm. The old lock keeper's cottage has been converted to a café.

Below Cowley Peachey Junction marks the start of the five-mile-long Slough Arm. It opened in 1882, making it one of the last canals to be built in Britain. The main reason for its construction was to transport bricks to central London from the huge clay deposits in the Slough area. In later years the canal carried large amounts of gravel dug from quarries in the same region.

Bottom The Paddington Packet Boat pub near Uxbridge is named after a passenger service which operated on the canal between Uxbridge and Paddington. The service began in 1801 and the horse-drawn boats would take about a day to complete the 15 mile journey.

Bulls Bridge

Main picture Bulls Bridge marks the junction of the Grand Union Main Line and the Paddington Arm. The boat in the picture is turning into the Paddington Arm, where it will have almost 14 miles of level cruising uninterrupted by locks. The Canal Company offices and repair yard were based at Bulls Bridge, making it an important place in the canal's working days. A large fleet of working narrow boats, was based here, carrying goods as varied as coal, timber, cocoa, grain and jam. Kearley & Tonge's jam factory, which was a few yards beyond the bridge, was known to the working boatmen as 'The Jam 'Ole'. It was the last company in London to receive regular supplies of coal by boat from the Midland coalfields. Bulls Bridge was a place where boatmen would stop and wait for orders while their wives would take advantage of the luxury of running water to do the family wash. The site is now a 24-hour supermarket with moorings for visiting boats.

Below Boating through the ice near Bulls Bridge. The factory in the background has been owned by Nestlé since 1929 and was once a regular user of the canal, taking coal from the Cannock coalfield in Staffordshire by canal boat. The working boatmen called it 'Hayes Cocoa'.

Hanwell

Main picture A pair of working narrowboats entering a lock on the Hanwell flight. Huge amounts of coal were brought down the Grand Union Canal from Midland collieries to fuel London's waterside industries. Regular traffic ended in the early 1960s but there are still a few enthusiasts keeping the tradition of carrying cargoes on the Canal. There are six locks in the Hanwell flight, followed by two more above Three Bridges. A bricked up arch along the flight marks the place where a canal arm went into the former County Lunatic Asylum. Coal was delivered to fuel the hospital boilers. The adjacent lock is still known as 'Asylum Lock'.

Below In 1859, one of Isambard Kingdom Brunel's last assignments was to build a railway line from the Great Western Main Line at Southall down to Brentford Dock. At Windmill Lane in Southall he created a railway, road and canal crossing now known as Three Bridges. Here the Grand Union Canal crosses the railway on a cast iron aqueduct. The top lock on the Hanwell flight can be seen in the background. In 1810, JMW Turner painted a sunset scene called 'Southall Mill'. The windmill in the painting has long gone but it would have stood near the lock above Three Bridges. It has bequeathed its name to today's Windmill Lane.

Osterley

Main picture The canal-side headquarters of GlaxoSmithKline at Great West Road, Brentford is a striking modern waterside building. It stands next to Boston Manor, which is a Tudor mansion dating from 1622. Boston Manor is open to the public on weekends during the summer months.

Below Osterley House was first built in 1576 but was modernised by Robert Adam in 1761. The Earl of Jersey opened it to the public in 1939 and gave it to the National Trust ten years later. Osterley is renowned for its Adam interiors, a 16th century stable block and a 350-acre landscaped park with a lake.

Bottom Gallows Bridge, Osterley, is a cast-iron turnover bridge which allowed horses towing working boats to cross the canal without being unhitched when the towpath changed sides. The bridge was built by the Horseley Iron Works company in Birmingham in 1820. Bridges like this are common on the midland canals but Gallows Bridge is the only one this far south. It acquired its name because of a gallows that once stood nearby where highwaymen and thieves were hanged.

Brentford

Main picture Thames Lock, Brentford, marks the entrance of the Grand Union Canal from the Thames. The lock is controlled by a lockkeeper, who checks the boat owner's licence for navigation on British Waterway's canals. The lock can only be used when the tide on the river is at the correct height.

Above left The Gauging Lock at Brentford with its attendant toll house. In the canal's commercial heyday, Brentford Depot was a centre of intense activity that steadily declined after the 1960s. The dock was surrounded by warehouses, which have now been demolished and replaced by modern housing and hotels. The listed toll house where boats' cargoes were assessed is a reminder of the depot's working past.

Left A fading plaque on the side of a waterside pub commemorates the fact that the artist JMW Turner lived in Brentford for three years.

Below The Boatmen's Institute at The Butts in Brentford was built in 1904 as a refuge for working canal boat families. Boating families lived on their boats and had a nomadic lifestyle. The institute was a place where they could leave their children for a short while, and it provided a rudimentary education.

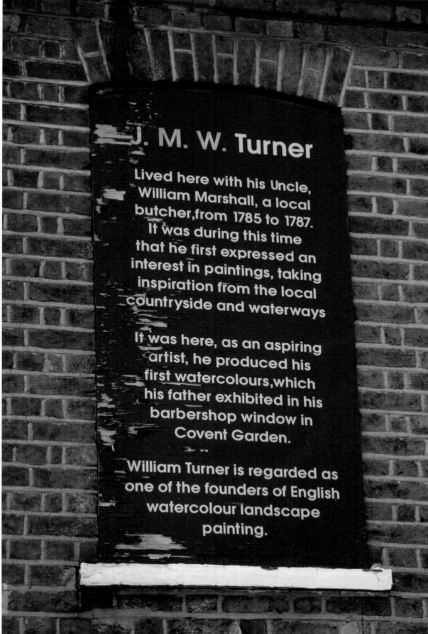

J. M. W. Turner

Lived here with his Uncle, William Marshall, a local butcher, from 1785 to 1787. It was during this time that he first expressed an interest in paintings, taking inspiration from the local countryside and waterways

It was here, as an aspiring artist, he produced his first watercolours, which his father exhibited in his barbershop window in Covent Garden.

William Turner is regarded as one of the founders of English watercolour landscape painting.

Syon Park

Syon House and its 200-acre park is the home of the Duke of Northumberland, whose family have lived here for over 400 years. It was founded as a medieval abbey over 500 years ago but was seized by Henry VIII. In 1547, Henry's body rested at Syon overnight en route to Windsor for burial. His remains leaked from the coffin and were partly eaten by dogs, fulfilling a prophesy that 'dogs would lick his blood' for his desecration of the abbey. Robert Adam redesigned the interior of the house in the 1760s and to this day it still contains some of his finest work. The park was landscaped by Capability Brown and the Great Conservatory was designed by Charles Fowler in the 1820s. Syon House, its grounds and garden centre are open to the public. A convenient side entrance to the park can be reached along the main road from the canal at Brentford Dock.

Main picture The Great Conservatory.

Below Syon House.

Bottom The lake at Syon House.

The Paddington Arm – Yeading to Northolt

Main picture Winter sunset at Yeading. During the mid-1800s brick making was the major industry in this area of west London. Bricks were transported along the canal to central London where they were used for building purposes, especially in the construction of the London sewers. Barges returned with loads of domestic rubbish, which was used to fill the excavated brickfield pits. The bridge and towpath are part of the 20-mile-long Hillingdon Trail footpath.

Below Willowtree Marina is sited on a former dock, where bricks made from clay extracted from surrounding land were sent to London by canal. The marina has extensive moorings, facilities for visiting boats and a quayside bistro restaurant.

Bottom The 14th-century St Mary's church at Northolt stands on a hill overlooking a medieval village green. One former rector was the distinguished 16th century cleric Nicholas Ridley, who supported Lady Jane Grey's claim to the throne. As a result, Ridley was burnt at the stake as a heretic in the reign of Queen Mary I.

Horsenden Hill

Main picture Perivale Wood is a 27-acre nature reserve next to the canal. It is owned by the Selborne Society and has an open day in the Spring, when visitors can enjoy millions of blue-bells flowering in the woodland.

Below Springtime boating on the canal at the foot of Horsenden Hill, which is the highest point in West London. The views from the summit stretch as far as Canary Wharf and the North Downs. To reach the summit there is a walk through ancient woodland.

Bottom left Summer wildflowers by the canal near Paradise Fields, a large wetland area with ponds, reed beds and wild flower meadows. A footbridge over the canal connects Paradise Fields to Horsenden Hill.

Bottom right Horsenden Hill woodland in autumn. Horsenden Hill has a waterside visitor centre and golf course.

Park Royal

Main picture The present North Circular Road Aqueduct replaced an earlier structure when the road was widened in 1993. The first aqueduct opened in 1933, when the North Circular Road was built. When it was replaced there was the problem of stopping the heavy traffic on the North Circular Road during its construction. The problem was solved by building the new structure alongside the original and then slowly jacking it into position. The old aqueduct was then taken away with only a minimum disruption to traffic.

Below The Park Royal industrial estate developed after the First World War, when it became the centre for munitions factories. Famous companies like Guinness and Heinz opened factories that used the canal for transporting raw materials and finished products. Park Royal is one of Europe's largest industrial estates, currently employing around 40,000 people in many diverse industries. Unfortunately, the canal is no longer used for commercial purposes but is still important for local recreation and as a place where workers can relax in their lunch breaks.

Bottom A boat crosses the North Circular Aqueduct, which divides into two separate channels. The emblem on the aqueduct behind the steerer is the Middlesex Coat of Arms. Bushes and trees on the offside of the canal conceal hundreds of unsightly container units.

Kensal Green to Little Venice

Below A boat passes the entrance to Porto Bella Dock, which was once a council disposal centre for domestic rubbish. Carts would proceed up a ramp to a covered wharf where their contents were tipped into barges which were then taken to Hayes, West Drayton and Yeading to fill holes left behind by brickfield quarrying. The buildings have now been converted into offices and studios. The elevated apartments in the background were used as a base for the contestants in the BBC television show *The Apprentice*.

Right The canal passes the 72-acre Kensal Green cemetery, which is London's oldest burial ground.

It is the last resting place for a number of famous people including Isambard Kingdom Brunel, William Thackeray, Anthony Trollope, Wilkie Collins and Terence Rattigan. The wooded nature of the cemetery makes it a home for over 30 species of birds and other wildlife. Guided tours around the graveyard are available.

Far right Four separate ages of transport are represented in this aerial view of the elevated A40 Westway as it crosses the Great Western Railway, the London Underground Railway and the Paddington Canal. The 2.5-mile-long Westway, which took four years to build opened in July 1970.

Paddington Basin and Little Venice

Main picture A passenger trip boat at Little Venice. The boat is about to enter a triangular-shaped-pool, which is the junction of the Regent's Canal and the Paddington Arm. The wooded island in the centre of the pool is known as Browning's Island, named after the poet Robert Browning, who once lived nearby. The building behind the bridge was a toll house where cargoes were weighed and issued with a toll ticket. Little Venice stages the annual Canalway Cavalcade on the first weekend of May. This colourful gathering of canal boats has become an important feature of the London boating scene.

Below In its commercial heyday, Paddington Basin was a busy inland port. It was flanked by warehouses and stables for the numerous horses that pulled the boats in the days before motor propulsion. Trade declined following the building of the Regent's Canal in 1820 and expansion of the railways, although it stayed in business until the end of the Second World War. Now transformed into Paddington Waterside, it is one of the biggest urban developments in Europe. The huge commercial, retail and leisure development includes hotels and the headquarters of Marks & Spencer.

The Regent's Canal: Maida Hill

Main picture The start of the Regent's Canal at Little Venice. Colourful boats line the canal along Blomfield Road as far as Maida Hill Tunnel, which has a café situated above the entrance. The tunnel has no towpath so walkers have to follow signs on the streets. Soil excavated from the tunnel was used to build the nearby cricket ground at Lords.

Below The 'Upside Down House' at Lisson Grove has its entrance at street level while its lower floors are above the tunnel entrance.

Below Wrought iron sign over entrance to private moorings.

Bottom The London Waterbus approaches Lisson Grove Tunnel. The waterbus service runs along the Regent's Canal from Little Venice to Camden Lock, stopping at London Zoo. This is by far the best way to visit the Zoo, avoiding the possibility of long queues at the park entrance. The waterbus runs daily between April and October, with a weekend service in the winter months.

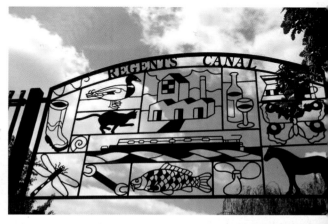

Snowdon A

Regent's Park

Main picture The Snowdon Aviary by the Regent's Canal at London Zoo was designed by photographer Lord Snowdon and opened in 1964. It was a landmark building because its aluminium framework allowed birds more space in which to fly.

Below The section of canal through Regent's Park is acknowledged to be one of the finest stretches of urban canal to be found anywhere in Britain. The bridge in the background of the picture is actually an aqueduct as it contains the River Tyburn within its masonry (see pages 150-151). Also in Regent's Park is Macclesfield Bridge, which is popularly known as 'Blow-Up Bridge'. In October 1874 a barge packed with gunpowder exploded under Macclesfield Bridge, killing the crew and totally destroying the bridge. The bridge was eventually rebuilt using the original columns, which were replaced back to front.

Bottom Passenger trip boat *Jenny Wren* passing London Zoo. The *Jenny Wren* is a daily service in the opposite direction to the Waterbus, starting at Camden Lock and turning at Little Venice.

Camden Lock

Main picture Most of the Regent's Canal locks were duplicated when the waterway was busy. Hampstead Road Lock at Camden is the only one left where both chambers are still in use. London's premier cosmopolitan market is centred around Hampstead Road Lock, popularly known as Camden Lock. The market is renowned for its arts and craft stalls, pubs and restaurants. Its colourful clothing shops mingle with exotic food stalls and boutiques for those with more adventurous tastes in clothes and jewellery.

Below Waterbuses in dock. These provide a regular service to Little Venice.

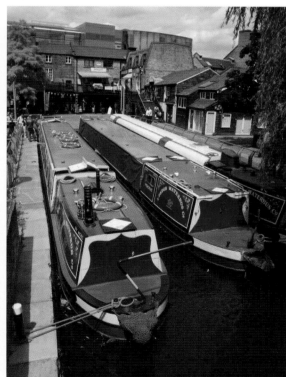

Camden Lock Market

Main picture Camden Lock Market attracts thousands of visitors from all over the world and has become one of London's top tourist attractions.

Below Headless chorus line.

Middle Food stalls.

Bottom Signs for sale.

Islington – King's Cross

Main picture The 960-yard-long Islington Tunnel is the longest canal tunnel in London. The approach to its eastern portal at City Road is through a beautiful wooded cutting overlooked by elegant terraced houses. There is no towpath so working boats had to be 'legged' through the tunnel while the boat horse was led over the top to the other side. 'Legging' required the boatmen to lie on a plank and propel the boat by walking along the tunnel wall. In 1826, a steam tug was employed to tow boats through the tunnel and this continued until boats with engines became commonplace.

Below King's Place, the latest addition to the London waterway scene, is situated opposite the London Canal Museum at Battlebridge Basin, King's Cross. It has the first new concert hall to open in London for over 25 years and is a centre for music and visual arts. King's Place has two art galleries with a restaurant and bars. Extensive office space above the halls is partly occupied by two national newspapers.

Bottom The London Canal Museum at Battlebridge Basin, King's Cross, is housed in a former ice warehouse. It was built in 1863 for Carlo Gatti who was a well known ice cream manufacturer. One of his ice wells has been preserved and can be seen in the museum. Visitors to the museum can learn about the history of London's canals and see a reconstructed boat cabin. There are displays of old photographs, canal art and a video of archive films.

Victoria Park

Main picture Victoria Park is flanked by both
Regent's and Hertford Union Canals. It was opened
in 1845 and is the largest open space in London's
east end. Popularly known as 'The People's Park' it
hosted many 19th-century political rallies. Today's
meetings are more likely to be rock concerts and
carnival processions. Victoria Park has a beautiful
lake close to Old Ford Lock, which features in the
picture. The Hertford Union Canal was built as a
short cut between the Regent's Canal and the River
Lee Navigation for boats wishing to avoid passing
through Regent's Canal Dock and the final locks
on the Regent's Canal.

Below In an intensely built up area like Hackney.
The canal plays a valuable role as a leisure outlet.
Here at Acton's Lock, cyclists ride by young
canoeists who are under instruction from an
expert adult.

Right Mile End Park was created from redundant
industrial land. It is a linear park following the
canal for about a mile. The park has an Ecology
Pavilion with a wetland area that is shown on the
picture.

Limehouse Basin

Main picture Limehouse Basin was previously known as Regent's Canal Dock. The dock opened in 1820 and had ten acres of water with four acres of quayside. It was very successful, handling produce and raw materials from all over the world, which were taken by canal boats for distribution throughout England. The dock also played an important role bringing coal brought down by canal from the Midland collieries. It remained active into the 1960s but despite the construction of a new tidal lock it closed to shipping in 1970. Limehouse Basin is now a marina surrounded by new luxury apartments and is the headquarters of the Cruising Association. The entrance to the Regent's Canal can be seen through the right hand arch, which supports the Dockland Light Railway.

Below The Ragged School Museum is situated by the canal in old warehouses between Mile End and Limehouse. Founded by Doctor Barnardo in 1877, this was the largest free school for poor children in London. The museum opened in 1990 and features a Victorian classroom, an East End kitchen and photographs showing life in Victorian East London. The museum is run by volunteers and relies on donations from visitors.

Bottom A Victorian East End kitchen at the Ragged School Museum.

River Lee Navigation

The River Lee Navigation, which runs from Hertford to the Thames, has three connections to the national waterway system. The Hertford Union Canal links the navigation to the Regent's Canal at Old Ford, allowing boats to avoid Limehouse Basin and three locks. The one-mile-long Limehouse Cut connects the Lee to Limehouse Basin at Bow Locks and the natural tidal river finally feeds into the Thames at Bow Creek.

The Bow Back Rivers consist of a maze of tidal channels between Bow and Stratford. They were once important in providing water for industry and powering mills. In recent years most of the local industry disappeared leaving behind a redundant region of neglected waterways that had silted up and their banks had become overgrown. Now restoration is under-way as they will form an integral part of the 2012 Olympic Park. A new lock near Three Mills has been built to provide water access for construction materials to the Olympic site. During the Games, visitors will be able to walk along the foot-paths and take boat trips around the Olympic Park.

The Lee Valley Regional Park stretches for 25 miles along the banks of the River Lee from Ware in Hertfordshire to the Thames at East India Dock Basin. The Park offers many outdoor activities such as rowing, boating and angling on the river and sailing on the adjacent lakes and reservoirs. Its numerous nature reserves are also popular with walkers and bird-watchers. The Park is particularly important in its lower reaches where it provides a green corridor through the urban sprawl of London's East End.

Other attractions include the Lee Valley Leisure Complex at Pickett's Lock, where there is an indoor athletics centre, golf course, multi-screen cinemas, caravan park, restaurants and bars. There is also the Markfield Beam Engine Museum at Tottenham, which has a restored steam engine that was originally installed here in 1883 to pump sewage to the works at Beckton. It is a splendid example of Victorian public-health engineering and is open to the public on special steaming days. Another big attraction in the Lee Valley is the Royal Gunpowder Mills at Waltham Abbey. Here you can learn all about the history of explosives and walk through a beautiful 170-acre site that incorporates a nature reserve. Events at the Gunpowder Mills include medieval jousting and re-enactments of historic battles.

Waltham Town Lock is situated near the Royal Gunpowder Mills and marks the place where the Lee Valley Park begins to open out into the countryside.

Three Mills

Main picture The House Mill at Three Mills was built in 1776 and is Britain's largest remaining tide mill. Built across the River Lea, the mill trapped water at high tide and then released it on the ebb to turn the water wheels. The mill stopped work in 1941 after it was bombed by enemy planes. The House Mill, along with the Clock Mill, are listed buildings in a conservation area. The clock on the Clock Mill is actually older than the mill itself. A third mill was wind operated, but it no longer exists.

Top right Abbey Mills was originally built in the 1860s as part of Sir Joseph Bazalgette's drainage scheme for London. It is one of the largest pumping stations in the UK and a fine example of Victorian industrial architecture. The modern Abbey Mills has multiple parallel pumps and can be operated by just one person.

Far right The main 25,000 seat Olympic stadium under construction in June 2009. Until recently, the Bow Back Rivers were a series of quiet backwaters

off the River Lea between Bow and Stratford. Now these channels are forming the watery centrepiece of the 2012 Olympic Games.

Near right City Mill Lock was built in the 1930s as part of a plan to upgrade the Bow Back Rivers. Unfortunately it was little used and eventually became derelict. The lock has now been restored with new gates and will play its part in the regeneration of the Bow Back Rivers as part of London's Olympic Park.

Lee Valley

Main picture The Lee Navigation near Pickett's Lock. Here the navigation is bordered on one side by a large reservoir, with a leisure complex on the opposite side. The Lee Valley Leisure Centre at Pickett's Lock is home to an athletics centre, golf course, multi-screen cinemas, restaurants and a caravan site.

Below Anglers withdraw their rods as a boat enters Stonebridge Lock. The Lea has long been a favourite river for anglers since Isaak Walton wrote his classic book *The Compleat Angler* in 1653.

Most locks on the Lee Navigation are mechanised and paired except for Pickett's, which is single and manually operated.

Bottom In 1866, 4,000 people in East London died in a cholera epidemic, mainly due to the pollution of the River Lea. This led to the Markfield treatment works at Tottenham that opened in 1886 and worked until 1964, when it was no longer required. The original steam-driven beam engine has been restored and the Markfield museum is open to the public on special steaming days.

Waltham Abbey

Main picture The Abbey Church at Waltham Abbey. The present church represents about half of the original Norman buildings which were destroyed by the Dissolution in 1540. What has survived is regarded as one of the finest examples of Norman architecture in the country. Also notable is a 14th-century chapel and the west tower built in 1556. The Abbey was founded in 1030 and consecrated in 1060 by Harold before the Battle of Hastings. A memorial to King Harold is said to be on the site of his burial place in the former chancel of the original abbey, now destroyed.

Below Fishers Green near Waltham Abbey is enjoyed by both walkers and birdwatchers in the Lee Valley Country Park. In 2003, 25,000 reeds were planted in the lake to increase the reed beds by 11 acres. A Bittern Information Point has cameras placed within the reed beds to allow visitors a chance to observe wintering bitterns. The Lee Valley Park wetlands are one of the main inland wintering areas for birds in Britain, annually supporting over 10,000 waterbirds.

Enfield and Gunpowder Mills

Main picture The Royal Small Arms Factory at Enfield, which closed towards the end of the 1990s. In 1907, the Lee Enfield rifle was introduced and subsequently became the main infantry weapon used in two world wars. It is estimated that over five million rifles were made at Enfield. It is widely believed that the name Lee is derived from the nearby river but it was probably named after its American designer James Lee. The factory has now been transformed into the Enfield Island Village, which houses an estimated population of around 3,000 people. The building with the clock tower is one of the few surviving original buildings.

Below The Royal Gunpowder Mills at Waltham Abbey. Gunpowder had been made here since the 1660s, before the mills acquired the royal title in 1787. It was abandoned by the Ministry of Defence in 1981 and opened to visitors in 2001. Water from the River Lea powered the mills and specially-designed boats carried gunpowder around the huge site on five miles of canals. The semi circular bridge in the picture allowed high-arched gunpowder boats to pass underneath. Today's visitors can learn everything about the history of gunpowder.

Bottom A battle re-enactment by the Medieval Siege Society at the Royal Gunpowder Mills.

London's Other Waterways

The Thames is fed by several tributaries within the London area. Over 100 miles of rivers and streams once flowed through meadows and villages on their way to the Thames. As London's population expanded, the villages turned into towns and the rivers became polluted with sewage. Industry brought further problems and the resulting effluent eventually ended up in the Thames. It was not understood that cholera and other waterborne diseases were directly attributed to polluted water and it is estimated that 10,000 Londoners died of cholera in 1854. 1858 was the year of the Big Stink when pollution on the Thames almost closed Parliament.

Sir Joseph Bazalgette was appointed chief engineer of the Metropolitan Board of Works in 1856 and he began work on a system of underground sewers, which took ten years to complete. Several rivers on both sides of the Thames disappeared underground to be diverted through culverts into the new sewerage system. Here they were intercepted before reaching the Thames and diverted to new treatment works. Bazalgette then built embankments alongside the river which covered the sewers, reclaimed ground for riverside roads and protected central London from flooding. This elaborate system of interconnected brick sewers is still in use today.

Among the rivers that vanished beneath the streets were the Fleet, the Westbourne, the Tyburn, the Effra and the Neckinger. Some of these lost rivers could be brought back to the surface as part of a plan to create more open spaces and water features. However, ideas such as turning Fleet Street into a Venetian-style waterway would be costly and extremely impractical.

The River Lea is the most important of the surviving visible tributaries followed by the Brent, the Wandle and the Roding. Other streams and small rivers that can be followed by foot include the Crane and Beverley Brook, which takes an attractive course through Richmond Park. There is also the New River, which isn't a river at all but an artificial waterway created to bring water from springs in Hertfordshire to London.

The Welsh Harp, also known as the Brent Reservoir, was formed in the 1830s when the River Brent was dammed. Apart from supplying water it also acted as feeder for the Grand Union Canal. It became a fashionable resort for Londoners in Victorian Times and even had its own station. The rowing events of the 1948 London Olympics were held here and since then it has become an important nature reserve and sailing area. The Welsh Harp was named after a local pub that no longer exists.

Brent River Park

Main picture   The Wharncliffe Viaduct viewed from Hanwell Bridge. Built in 1837 by Isambard Kingdom Brunel, the viaduct carries the Great Western Railway from London to Bristol. There is also a regular service between Heathrow Airport and Paddington Station. It is said that Queen Victoria instructed her Royal Train driver to stop on the viaduct so she could admire the view. The present bridge over the Brent at Hanwell, which was erected in 1762, has been widened over the years. In 1973, the Brent River & Canal Society was founded by Luke FitzHerbert to campaign for the creation of a continuous 4.5-mile park alongside the River Brent. The Brent River Park eventually opened in 1975 with local council funding. The walk extends from the A40 near Hanger Lane to Brentford High Street, incorporating the Grand Union Canal towpath at Hanwell Locks. Brent Lodge Park known locally as Bunny Park has a small zoo, roaming peacocks, a millennium maze and an excellent cafe.

Below   A beautiful section of the River Brent from Hanwell Bridge to the locks is called FitzHerbert Walk after the BRCS founder. The Brent River Park is now part of the Capital Ring long distance footpath that encircles the whole of London.

Above   St Mary's Church at Hanwell. There is evidence of a 10th-century church on this site that was rebuilt in the 12th century. The present church was built by George Gilbert Scott in 1842. It has wall paintings by the artist William Yeames, who was a churchwarden at the time and lived in Hanwell.

River Wandle

Main picture The present parkland at Morden Hall was created around 1860. Morden Hall was built in 1770, replacing the original manor house called Growtes. During the First World War the hall became a military hospital. Morden Hall park is now owned by the National Trust and is open to the public.

Near right In the 1830s, Liberty imported plain silks from India and had them printed at Merton Abbey Mills. The silk printing at Merton lasted until 1972 although textile printing continued on the site for some years later. In the 1880s, William Morris designed and printed wallpapers, woven textiles and carpets at Merton Abbey. The William Morris company also designed and produced stained glass at Merton. Today, Merton Abbey Mills is an arts and crafts market with a riverside pub and restaurants.

Top right The 18th-century Snuff Mill at Morden Hall used to grind tobacco into powder after it had been dried in kilns. It is now used as an Environmental Study Centre for children.

Bottom right The seven spoke waterwheel at Merton Abbey Mills is London's only working example of a waterwheel. The Liberty workshops used it to drive spools to rinse silk after gumming and printing.

River Roding

Main picture The reedy Barking Creek near the flood barrier that marks its junction with the River Thames. In September 1878, the *Princess Alice* paddle steamer sank with over 750 people aboard after a collision with the large collier *Bywell Castle* at Gallions Reach near the entrance to Barking Creek. 700 people were drowned and it represents the biggest inland shipping disaster in Britain.

Right The Curfew Tower Gatehouse at Barking. Built in 1460, this is all that remains of Barking Abbey, which was dissolved and destroyed in 1541 during the reign of Henry VIII. The Abbey dated back to AD666 and was the headquarters of William the Conqueror after his coronation. The Gatehouse, now forms the entrance to St Margaret's Church, where Captain Cook was married in 1762.

Below River Roding at Barking Wharf. This was once an important base for a large fishing fleet and it also shipped timber for the navy from nearby Epping Forest.

New River

Main picture The New River by the West Reservoir at Stoke Newington. Two reservoirs were built at Stoke Newington in the 1830s to meet the rising demand for water. Today, only the East Reservoir is used for storing water while the West Reservoir has become a water sports centre.

Right The New River passes through the north-east corner of Finsbury Park.

Below In the reign of Elizabeth I London's population had grown to such an extent that its rivers had become dangerously polluted. The New River, which opened in 1603, brought fresh water to the City from Hertfordshire. It is an artificial waterway travelling 38 miles along a natural land contour dropping six inches every mile, thus relying on gravity to reach its destination. The original terminus was at Islington but now the river ends at a reservoir at Stoke Newington. The building in the photograph is Castle Pumping Station at Green Lanes, Stoke Newington. It was built in 1855 but is no longer required for its original purpose and has been converted to an indoor climbing centre.

Middle This late-18th-century brick watch hut at Canonbury Grove was once used by linesmen for storage and shelter. The redundant New River channels at Canonbury Grove have become part of a public garden walk.

River Crane

Main picture Woodland walk by the River Crane. Crane Park, which has extensive woodland by the river, was made into a nature reserve in 1990. The river eventually joins the Thames near Eel Pie Island in Twickenham.

Below The Shot Tower in Crane Park, Hanworth. The River Crane was known as 'The Powder Mill River' because of the manufacture of gunpowder by its banks. The Shot Tower is all that remains of a large powder mill built around 1767. Gunpowder mills were established on Hounslow Heath in the early 16th century and many more were added during the reign of Elizabeth I. The site at Crane Park, which once covered over 100 acres, remained in business until 1927 when it lost its licence to make gunpowder and closed. Population growth in the area made the site unsuitable because of the risk of explosions.

Below The Yeading Brook at Roxbourne Park, Ruislip. This section is noted for its wildflowers and diverse insect population. This little stream becomes the River Crane at Cranford Park.

River Tyburn

Main picture In 1812, architect John Nash diverted the River Tyburn to feed the lake in his newly created Regent's Park. The river, which is now almost entirely underground, follows a meandering course from Hampstead to the Thames. At a point near what is now St James's Park it split into three branches, two of which formed the island of Thorney, where Westminster Abbey was built. It also gave its name to the Tyburn Gallows which was erected on a site near Marble Arch. A pivotal scene in David Lean's classic film *Brief Encounter* between Trevor Howard and Celia Johnson was filmed on the lake in Regent's Park.

Above right Grays Mews Antique Market in Davies Street, Mayfair was opened in 1977 on the site of the former John Bolding water closet manufacturers. It now has around 80 dealers inside the building. The River Tyburn runs through the basement with goldfish happily swimming in it. Nearby Oxford Street was originally called Tyburn Road after the river.

Below right The River Tyburn runs through Bridge 8 on the Regent's Canal. The 'V' shaped groove on the arch beneath the bridge appears to channel the little river into Regent's Park.

River Westbourne

Main picture The Serpentine Bridge in Hyde Park was built in 1824 by George Rennie.

Top The Italian Fountains at the end of the Serpentine in Kensington Gardens have become favourite locations for film and television companies.

Bottom The Westbourne crosses the District Line underground station at Sloane Square inside a large pipe. The Westbourne River begins its life near the western source of the Fleet on Hampstead Heath.

It flows through Kilburn and Paddington before feeding the Serpentine lake in Hyde Park. On the orders of Queen Caroline the river was dammed in 1730 to form the Serpentine. Most of the river remained open until the mid-1800s when, like the Fleet, it had become severely polluted as London's population expanded and it disappeared underground. Fashionable Knightsbridge derives its name from a bridge over the Westbourne, which in the 16th century was notorious as a haunt of highwaymen.

River Neckinger

Main picture The River Neckinger enters the Thames at St Saviour's Dock near Tower Bridge. It is said that the name Neckinger refers to a place where pirates were hanged by a rope called the Devil's Neckcloth (Neckinger). It was a squalid area in Victorian times, described in 1849 as 'The Venice of Drains' and 'The Capital of Cholera'. Dickens used Jacobs Island as a location in *Oliver Twist*.

Right Jacob's Island plaque.

Fleet

Main picture The River Fleet near its eastern source at Hampstead Heath. It has two sources, one of which fills the Hampstead Ponds and the other which fills the Highgate Ponds. Afterwards the river unites and disappears underground, making it the largest subterranean river in London. In medieval times the river was very much on the surface and marked the boundary between the cities of London and Westminster. In 1680, Sir Christopher Wren, architect of St Paul's Cathedral, converted the lower reaches into a canal that lasted a mere 50 years because the tolls were too high. Most of the river degenerated into an open sewer and in 1846 one section actually exploded because of foul gases from the pollution. As London developed the river was buried underground and in 1872 it was diverted into the interceptory sewer.

Below Fleet Street sign.

When a man is tired of London, he is tired of life.

'Why, Sir, you find no man at all intellectual, who is willing to leave London. No, Sir, when a man is tired of London, he is tired of life; for there is in London all that life can afford.'

Samuel Johnson

Index

Acknowledgements

To my old friend Tony Ellis, former editor of
Thames Guardian magazine, who was supplying
me with information only two weeks before his
untimely death in 2008.

To Ann and Llewellyn for inviting me to join them
on a memorable cruise on the Thames by sailing
barge.

To Paul Tritton for information supplied following
his wanderings along some of London's lesser
known waterways.

To my wife Janet who accompanied me on many
of my waterway explorations.

For supplying information or providing
access, many thanks to:
Ed Fox at British Waterways, London
Roger Squires at The London Canal Museum
Brick Lane Music Hall, Silvertown
Ragged School Museum, Mile End
The Kew Bridge Steam Museum

And thanks to the National Trust, English Heritage
and other organisations whose properties feature
in this book.

Also to Fred Barter for his design skills and
enthusiasm in the production of this book.

Finally to Liz Piercy at Adlard Coles Nautical
with whom it has been such a pleasure to work on
this book.

Published by Adlard Coles Nautical
an imprint of A & C Black Publishers Ltd
36 Soho Square, London W1D 3QY
www.adlardcoles.com

Copyright © Derek Pratt 2010

First edition 2010

ISBN 978 1-4081-1074-4

A CIP catalogue record for this book is available from the
British Library.

This book is produced using paper that is made from
wood grown in managed, sustainable forests. It is natural,
renewable and recyclable. The logging and manufacturing
processes conform to the environmental regulations of
the country of origin.

Typeset in 10pt Minion.
Printed and bound in Singapore by Star Standard

Designed by Fred Barter at Bosun Press